SUMERIANS

THE LAND OF THE CIVILISED KINGS

DISCOVER THE TRUTH ABOUT THE SUMERIANS

Babylonia, Nibiru, Gilgamesh & Planet X

Michael Hector

© 2016

COPYRIGHT NOTICE

DISCLAIMER

Although the author and publisher have made every effort to ensure that the information in this book was correct at press time, the author and publisher do not assume and hereby disclaim any liability to any party for any loss, damage, or disruption caused by errors or omissions, whether such errors or omissions result from negligence, accident, or any other cause.

This book is not intended as a substitute for the medical advice of physicians. The reader should regularly consult a physician in matters relating to his/her health and particularly with respect to any symptoms that may require diagnosis or medical attention.

TABLE OF CONTENTS

INTRODUCTION

In the fourth millennium before Christ there was a culture known as the Sumerians; they are known as one of the earliest civilisations in the world, in fact many people see them as the first. The land of Sumer lies where Iraq and Kuwait now stand; it was originally known as the southern tip of Mesopotamia. In many ways the civilisation seems to have appeared from nowhere. There have been many theories regarding this sudden existence and this book will look at some of the most common beliefs; both those believed to have been held by the Sumerians and those held today.

The society is also responsible for many modern beliefs, including alien activity! There was widespread worship of the gods and it is even believed that the Sumerians were able to see objects in space, such as Planet X; a phenomena which is still talked about today. The word Sumer is part of the ancient Akkadian language and literally means 'Land of the Civilised Kings'. The land they occupied was simply referred to as the land and they were known simply as the black headed people.

Their culture has spawned two great cities; Uruk which is widely regarded as the oldest city in the world and Eridu which the Sumerians regarded as the oldest city. The Sumerians believe that the city of Eridu was given to them by the gods along with all the skills necessary to form civilised culture. Whichever city is actually the oldest does not change the fact that this is seen as the first real civilisation in the world.

It is important to note that the Sumerians were not the first people to settle on this land. Relatively recent evidence has arisen which suggests that the area was originally occupied by a society known as Ubaid. Scientists have been unable to confirm where these early humans arrived from but the variety of artefacts which have been found suggest that they had already given up a nomadic lifestyle and were living as farmers. There have been a variety of tools, including hoes and knives made from stone which are older than 5000BC. Historians are still unable to calculate exactly when this society either developed into the Sumerians or was replaced by it.

As the first civilisation there is a range of documents dating from this period which help to provide an insight into how the civilisation evolved and what concepts were created which have been carried through to the modern world. Unfortunately, the information which has been recorded does little to illuminate the history of this period. Much of the information known has been gleaned from the archaeological and geological records of this time period.

What has been established is that the Sumerian civilisation lasted from 5000Bc to 1750BC. At this point the Sumerians were invaded and defeated by the Elamites and the Amorites. The early part of this civilisation is thought to have lasted from 5000BC to 4100BC and is the part now referred to as the Ubaid society. It was this society which formed several villages; these became cities under the Sumerians. The Sumerians were a mighty force during this period; many cities were developed; including the already mentioned Uruk and Eridu. It is believed that Uruk was the largest and most powerful of all the cities. It was also during this period that the idea of trading with foreign countries first came to prominence. It is believed that this trade was the general reason why a good method of writing was established; it was essential to ensure communication between all the different cultures.

It is interesting to note that the Sumerians were ruled by a monarch and that this monarch was supported by a group of advisors; these were known as the council of elders and consisted of men and women. The Sumerians based their civilisation on a belief in the gods and that human civilisation was only possible because the gods had managed to make order out of chaos. Their society lasted for over three thousand years and saw some remarkable advancement in culture and technology.

It is possible to break the Sumerian period into several distinct sections; the first chapter of this book deals with this, including the natural progression and evolvement. There is also a section which deals with the rise of Gilgamesh, the fifth king of Uruk; he is believed to be a demi-god with superhuman strength and lived for an impressive one hundred and twenty six years. The book also deals with how the legend of Planet X (also known as Nibiru) ties into the Sumerian culture and how this myth is still alive today. Alongside this it is believed that the Sumerians were the predecessors of the Babylonian civilisation. This book looks into how the mighty Babylonians arose from the Sumerian dynasty and the links between both societies; with a particular emphasis on the advancements in culture and technology.

Finally, there are many theories and rumours surrounding the arrival of the Sumerians and their links with life from other planets. It is believed that they may even have been aliens and choose to settle on this planet for a time. There are a variety of facts which help to garnish interest in this statement and belief; these include the tablets, ancient Sumerian texts and just how advanced their civilisation was. They appear to have a good level of knowledge regarding the solar system and the calendars which were created during this period still exist today; in common use. Even their mathematical concepts are relevant today. This book will look at the facts regarding their existence and origin; the possibility of the Sumerians being an alien life force or that the gods they refer to were actually the aliens guiding them and offering them a better life. The Sumerians were devoted to their gods and believed that they were created in their likeness; a concept that the main religions of today also embrace; although they arose after the time of the Sumerians.

CHAPTER 1 – THE HISTORY OF THE SUMERIANS

According to some extremely brief historical documents King Etana of Kish was the first official leader of the Sumerian people. It seems likely that he came to power early in the third millennium before Christ. The brief history summarises him as the king which stabilized the lands. He is recorded in the list of kings was created in approximately 2100 BC and shows every king of Sumer; it confirms the leaders and the continuity of this leadership throughout the Sumerian period. In fact, it is also believed that this list was created to authenticate the reign of Utu–Hegal of Uruk. The list represents him as the latest one in a long line of kings and demi-gods. By having himself added to the list it is thought he would be elevated to this status to at least the people of the land. Many of the other kings on the list were remembered for superhuman feats and Utu-Hegal clearly wanted the same memory for himself.

Although the exact date that the Sumerians arrived in the area is a mystery; it has been confirmed that the Sumerians did invent the wheel, had the ability to write in their own elaborate language, created sailing boats and even used advanced farming techniques, such as irrigation. There are even many documents which refer to their cities as the first concept of a city; although China and India both contest this claim.

The period between 4100 BC and 2900BC is known as the Uruk period and is the most prominent part of the Sumerian history. This period is known by the name of the city of Uruk as this was the largest and most powerful city; although the Sumerians always maintained that Eridu was the first city to be formed. Although the area was formed into smaller states, all of them responded to a single King. It is interesting to note that all the kings which followed Etna were Semites; it is only the ninth king on the list who had a Sumerian name and more Sumerian kings followed.

The period between 2900 BC and 2334 BC saw a change in a King with priestly powers to a more modern day approach to Kingship. This shift was subtle yet dramatic as it emphasized the moving away from the religious beliefs that had been a huge part of their culture. The various cities within Sumer were internally fighting during this period as they all wanted the best arable land and the right to the water on the land. In fact, it took King Eannutum to unite the states. He came to power in 2500BC and built the first dynasty of Lagash. It is credited as being the forefather of the mighty Akkadian Empire. The Lagash Empire included the majority of Sumer and extended into what was known as Elam. The empire survived until the founding of the Akkadian Empire in 2234 BC, by a man called Sargon of Akkad. In fact, this empire is known as the first example of a multinational empire. The empire included Sumer as well as the majority of Mesopotamia. Unfortunately it only survived for sixteen years before the invasion of the Gutians. This invasion destroyed many of the modern cities and took control of the Sumer region until 2047 BC. The Gutians were not well received or well liked by the Sumerians and there are many texts which testify to their feelings towards these people.

Finally in 2047 BC the Sumerian Renaissance period started. This period lasted until the end of the Sumerian's in 1750 BC. Each of the kings during this period opted for peace between the states and pushed to advance culture, the arts and even entertainment. The range of tools and other creations that appeared during this time have left historians with little doubt as to the importance of this era in human development. They are also the reason behind many of the modern day alien theories. This part of history is credited with having the first proverbs, the first schools and even the first love song. In fact, this period is also credited with the first legal precedents and the first moral ideas.

Perhaps most importantly, it was the Sumerians who segmented time with their counting system. Their system was based upon the number sixty which is why there is sixty seconds in a minute and sixty minutes in an hour. There concept of time extended to an understanding of night and day; twelve hours of each and the working day. Alongside this there is even the idea that people, should have holiday days. This concept of time still exists today!

There are a range of legal concepts which came into effect during this time; these are recorded by several historians and point to the fact that the kings during this period sort to regulate every aspect of life. It is commonly accepted that this stage of the Sumerian dynasty is known as the patrimonial stage. This is the idea that the entire state is led by one father figure who guides his people along the best path to prosperity and happiness. These concepts and the desire to set examples led King Shulgi to run the one hundred miles between Ur, the capital and Nippur; the religious centre of his empire. Historians have ascertained it would have been possible and, in fact, would have been in keeping with his style of rule.

His final legacy was a wall one hundred and fifty five miles long which was designed to keep the neighbouring barbaric tribes out. Unfortunately, although this was strengthened and by subsequent generations, it was breached in 1750 and the king was carried away when the city of Ur was over run. The subsequent famine which resulted from the change in farming methods and over use of the land meant that many people left this area and moved further south. In a very short space of time the Sumerian culture vanished as the cities were over run and the Sumerians scattered. However, many of the developments of this period are still in existence today and testify to the advanced thinking of this once great culture.

The Sumerian civilisation which occupied this area for such a long period of time seemed to have appeared from nowhere and vanished just as quickly. It is this combination of factors which has led many to suggest that the culture was either alien in nature or a product of alien intervention on Earth. Why these aliens chose to intervene and then disappear is a mystery that may never be solved. What is interesting is that there are only theories as to how the Sumerians came to occupy this stretch of land; no records appear to exist regarding this.

It is apparent that the Sumerians enjoyed creating and using pottery; there are literally hundreds of styles of bowls which date from this period; many of them are made for specific purposes; such as for honey, butter or even oil. There is also evidence of feather head-dresses, beds, stools and even chairs. Weapons include drills, knives, daggers, and even bows and arrows. There were even primitive saws. Writings were generally recorded on tablets and there, appears to be a love of music. The majority of cultures at this time were male dominated; however, the Sumerians were much more advanced in their attitudes towards women. Women or men were either free or slaves; a free woman would be a daughter, then a wife and then, if they outlived their husband, they would be a widow but free to marry again.

One of the most exciting parts of the Sumerian culture is their ability to write in their own language; this are numerous clay tablets which have been discovered and these all testify to the ability of ancient man to create works of art as well as simple records. The Sumerian language is not the oldest in the world but it is a milestone in human development. Having said that it can be difficult, even for an expert to translate some of the earliest text as the language bears little resemblance to language formats of today. There are many traces of this language in the Akkadian language which is known to have replaced Sumerian. Today Sumerian is an ancient language which is only read or written; much as Latin is.

The Sumerian culture was divided into many states and each state worshipped its own god. There appears to be two different approaches to this belief. The first is that creation was a result of several marriages between the gods; opposites were brought together to create divine beings. This theory postulated through all of the Sumerian society; meaning that many other things in society were seen as a merging of opposites; such as fresh water and sea water. The second approach sees the gods needing humans to do the manual chores on earth; as such they created humans from clay and brought them to life; with the sole purpose of serving them. This is the theory that is easily adapted to suit those who believe that the Sumerians were actually aliens; or controlled by them.

This theory is taken a stage further as the Sumerians appear to have detailed maps of the solar system and the stars around earth. They are believed to be the first civilisation to have attempted this type of undertaking and many of the constellations they discovered and named still exist today. These are commonly known as the signs of the zodiac and were embraced by the Greek culture before becoming part of modern day life. The Sumerians recorded that there are five planets; these are the ones which can be seen by the naked eye. However, some of their writings refer to the ten planets in the solar system which many believe is a reference to the mysterious Planet X. What is certainly puzzling is how they could have known about the existence of all the planets in the solar system when they are not visible to either the naked eye or the technology which was in existence at this time.

Even basic mathematics can be traced back to this period; the Sumerians used several different systems and alternating between a base of six and ten. Some of these concepts are still used today. In addition, possibly due to the extended period of war which was experienced between this culture and their neighbours, the Sumerians can be credited with having a highly disciplined military strategy and enlisted soldiers. There are records of them marching into battle with shields, helmets and in a standard formation; something that no regular army would have done at this time.

The Sumerians are also noted as one of the earliest civilisations to use intensive farming methods; these were particularly effective at the time with Emmer wheat, barley and even sheep farming. This combined with new irrigation methods to ensure that crops were always in plentiful supply and even cattle were kept for the sole purpose of meat; on a much larger scale than had ever been seen before.

There are certainly questions raised as to how this primitive society managed to make so many advancements in their technological and cultural practices. Many of their advancements bore no relation to the other practices in place at this time and lead to the question of what was their secret. Even the wheel has been shown to originate from this culture; first as a pottery wheel and then quickly adapted for transport use. Whether this was a result of good leaders who focused on developing and improving the lives of their subjects, or, whether it was related to outside influences; we may never know. Certainly their achievements were impressive and have led to a variety of theories and possibilities which will continue to be discussed for years to come.

CHAPTER 2 – THE LEGEND OF NIBIRU

The vast steps forward in technology, culture and the arts may have another cause. There are those that have theorised that the Sumerians, who seemed to appear from nowhere, actually came from somewhere other than Earth. The fact that they effectively created a civilisation where none previously existed is enough to make you consider that this might be more than just another legend. There are other theories which suggest that the Sumerians were actually created by aliens simply to serve their needs; this may be as simple as mining gold or to provide for the aliens whilst they fixed a fault with their own craft. Of course; much of this is conjecture; it is very difficult to prove the existence of an alien race; especially one that may have visited the planet five or six thousand years ago.

The planet of Nibiru has been spoken about many times over the years, especially at specific moments during the build up to 2003 when it was believed that Planet X; an alternative name for Nibiru; might strike earth and cause a massive amount of damage; potentially even wiping out life as we know it. Of course, this did not happen. However, what is interesting is that the Sumerians knew there were twelve planets in our solar system. This is not in keeping with the current number of planets! In ancient times several stars were counted as planets; mainly because of the lack of ability to see these planets properly, or even to distinguish them from the other stars in our galaxy. These were included in the list of planets giving eleven planets in total. More recently, up until 2006 it was believed that there are nine planets in our solar system. However, in 2006 Pluto was reclassified as a dwarf planet so the official count now sits at eight. Whichever way you look at the figures, the Sumerians knew of an additional planet which is still unknown to us today. Nibiru, now commonly referred to as Planet X, is a massive planet in a three thousand six hundred year orbit. The last time this planet passed by Earth was supposed to have been in 2003. Planet X is supposed to be in an elliptic orbit which means it is not a traditional circular orbit such as Earth; this makes its path irregular and allows it the potential to vary its route; this is the reason why it could crash into any of the other planets in the solar system. In fact, it is much bigger than any of the other planets.

The name Nibiru actually means 'Planet of crossing' and the Sumerians believed that its elliptical orbit eventually took it between Mars and Jupiter. In the process it caused a huge amount of disruption and even collided with a planet known as Tiamat. This planet split into two, one half shattered and caused the asteroid belt which still exists today whilst the other half became Earth. Of course, the Earth no longer looks like half a planet, evolution, gravitational pulls and time have caused the planet to slowly reform into the sphere we now live on. The process caused the separation of the land mass into the countries and continents we know today.

There are two elements to this theory which must be studied closer to discover if there is any truth in these events. The first is what evidence is available to support this premise and whether an additional planet could exist, in such a large scale orbit. The second is, assuming this is true what effect could it have on the planet today; it passed Earth thirteen years ago and won't be back for many thousands of years.

It is believed that Nibiru has its own burning moon which acts like a sun, providing warmth and light regardless of where it is in its orbit of our sun. The size of this planet is estimated to be twenty times bigger than Jupiter and there are those that suggest the Anunnaki, the inhabitants of

Nibiru visited Earth twenty five thousand years ago. At the time; primitive humans were not capable of understanding the knowledge these aliens were keen to share. The result was the creation of gods which knew facts and had amazing power, un-comprehensible to humanity. This theory is supported through the times of the Mayan, who also knew of the existence of Nibiru. Their stories tell of a dark shape which will be crossing Earth in the distant future; something that apparently happened in 2003.

There are many clues in the Sumerian history which point towards the existence of Planet X. For example, in Sumerian the number three thousand six hundred is represented by a big circle. A Sumerian text which refers to the reigns periods are all multiples of three thousand six hundred. Alongside these references to the orbit time of Planet X, there are also the hints in both Sumerian texts and the bible of the return of the kingdom of heaven. It is highly likely that these predictions are based on sightings of the planet Nibiru, something which was periodically possible in the sky depending upon its location in the solar system. Many of the ancient texts you can find refer to the upheavals and devastation which occurs every time the 12th planet crosses by the Earth; this is not necessarily something they would have witnessed in their lifetime and yet the events which have happened since do bear some resemblance to their theories. Were the Sumerians incredibly good at guessing the future or did they have access to information that is not available to us today?

It is interesting that the Sumerians had their own theory on how humans came into existence. The story tells of humanoid gods which ruled the Earth. However, these gods completed all the work toiling on the earth day after day. Then, one day they all informed Anu, the god of the gods, that it was simply too much. Anu's son Enki and his half sister Ninki volunteered to make a humanoid being in the likeness of the gods. This being would do the work for them. In order for this to happen one of the gods had to die and his blood and his body was mixed with clay. From this the first humans were created. It is also interesting that the first man was created in Eden. In Sumerian this simply means 'flat terrain, it is reputed to be the garden of the gods. It seems strange that the bible refers to the beginning of man in a very similar way and also references Eden. The story continues that humans were originally unable to reproduce themselves; this was adjusted by Enki, one of the gods, although it was not approved by his brother Enlil. This led to a bitter battle between the gods.

When you study this story further you will discover further similarities between the Sumerian theory of creation and the bible's story of creation. For instance, the bible refers to Adam and eve in the Garden of Eden and the fact that are not able to eat the apple. They eat the forbidden fruit and are cast out of the garden; effectively rejected by god. The Sumerians tell of Enlil who fought for the rights of humans; he wanted humans to have freedom and understand that they were mining the land for the gods. It has been argued that introducing humans to the truth and freedom is the same as what the snake did to Adam and Eve in the Garden of Eden; it helped them to see they were enslaved in a garden; when they were cast out they gained their freedom and were rejected by god. Whilst there are few facts to back up this version of events it is interesting that all of this happened before Jesus was born and yet have incredibly similar approaches to the creation of the world. This is not just a theory or an idea regarding how the Sumerians felt about the existence of humanity. This story is found on one of the clay tablets which can be date approximately 1600 BC and is recorded in the Sumerian language. This confirms the existence of the Sumerian approach to the creation of life.

By itself this may be considered to be an eerie coincidence. However, this is only one of the stories which bear a striking resemblance to the stories which can be fold in the bible. The tablets which have been found date from the time of the Sumerians include a variety of stories, such as the story of a great flood and the survival of humanity and the animals in a great ark. This leads to a simple question; are the stories in the bible simply a rewrite of previously known stories or are they both reflections of humanity? If they are a reference to the Sumerian stories, or if the Sumerians knew about what would happen in the future then you must ask yourself how much of these stories are simply legends and how much truth is there in them.

One conclusion you can reach is that the Annuaki were aliens with an excellent knowledge of genetics. This theory can be supported by the fact that science has now confirmed that a massive flood occurred approximately ten thousand years ago. This would have destroyed humanity had the ark not been present. This leads to the question of whether the ark was a wooden ship or an alien space craft.

A further point which arises from this argument is that, if humanity was the result of a genetic mutation by an alien species, where is the alien species now. The answers to this may never be known. However, there are approximately thirty one thousand clay tablets which date from the time of the Sumerians; they all reside in the British museum and yet most of the tablets have not been translated. This is because the Sumerian language is like no other on earth and the tablets are damaged and fragmented; making it difficult to locate any patterns and translate the tablets accurately.

It is probable that any alien species which arrived on Earth would be interested in the minerals that would have been freely available at the time; ancient human civilisations would simply not have had the capability for complex mining. There are those who believe that the gods which the Sumerian's worshipped were actually simply the scientific discovery team from Nibiru; their god like qualities were simply a side-effect of their advanced technology and apparent power. Although this theory has been dismissed by many there is now evidence to suggest that large scale gold mining was completed in parts of South Africa; although it is difficult to prove the mining was a result of an alien species, the limited technological abilities of ancient man will make you question how else to interpret the facts.

All of these theories point to the existence of an alien race which, at the very least, gave life to the Sumerians. The Sumerian knowledge of the solar system seems simply too great to exist from the information available at that time. One of the Sumerian clay tablets shows an image of the solar system. Of course, it is possible that this image is not supposed to be the solar system, but, its resemblance is uncanny. The tablet shows an extra two planets, it is possible that one of these is moon or even the relatively recently discovered Sedna the other one must be Nibiru; the path of its orbit clearly shows the distance it travels and why the planet is only visible at certain times. The simpler fact that this information should have been beyond the grasp of this civilisation leads to more questions; including how was it possible. Without being able to decode the majority of the tablets it is highly likely that the answer to this will never be found.

There are those who have managed to provide good reasons as to why the theory of Planet X cannot be true. One of the main concerns is that current understanding of physics makes it impossible for a planet to stay in an elliptic orbit. At some point the planet would have to either shoot off into space or settle into a standard orbit. Of course, if the human understanding of physics remains limited there may be a way for this to exist that humans simply cannot grasp at this stage in time. The other part of this counter argument looks at the visibility of the planet. It seems highly unlikely; although again, not impossible, that this massive planet is moving around our solar system and it has never been spotted by any of the world's huge telescopes, super computers, or even the astronauts in space. Of course, if the modern theories are correct and this orbit is impossible over a long period of time, it is possible that the Planet X has already been thrown out of the solar system and into space. This may be the reason that it is not visible to the naked eye; unfortunately it is difficult to locate a planet accurately when it is thousands of miles away, across the galaxy. Not knowing in which direction or when it spun out of its orbit complicates the matter as it becomes virtually impossible to know where we should be looking and whether the planet remains in one piece or is even still capable of supporting life forms of some description.

The tablets which reflect this additional planet may have been simply drawing and hypothesizing or may have absolutely no connection with the solar system. In fact, the Sumerians, like the majority of emerging civilisations, may simply have been looking at the sky to find divine inspiration. It is quite possible that the stories regarding Nibiru, or Planet X, have their foundations in little more than an attempt to believe there was something more to life than just existence. As already mentioned; it is simply not possible to confirm what the tablets were saying as humans have yet to unlock their secrets. It is possible that this is because the inhabitants of Nibiru were so much more advanced than humans and it is simply not possible to comprehend their language yet. However, it is also possible that these tablets represent human's first attempt at creating a written language which was used to express ideas as well as essential facts. The same theory could be applied to the cave drawings of ancient man; rudimental drawings, a message from another planet or simply an attempt at art.

Whilst it may not be possible to confirm the existence of a Planet X, it is also not possible to completely rule it out. This means that the theory, which has already received a large amount of attention, will continue to exist long into the future.

Chapter 3 – Alien Connections and Conspiracies

Planet X is simply one theory as to how the Sumerians managed to develop and advance rapidly; creating civilisation where there was previously none. However, there have been several other theories postulated which relate to the Sumerian's and their knowledge of other planets. One of the most common theories is that of the ancient astronauts. These were beings from another planet which visited Earth thousands of years ago; human are either the descendents of these beings although at this moment in time, we are unable to comprehend the sheer mass of knowledge that was available to our alien ancestors. It seems unlikely that this theory could be true; if we are descendants of a species which is capable of travelling in space then how have we avoided retaining any of this knowledge through the generations.

The more likely scenario is that humans have evolved slowly and that aliens who have visited have shared some ideas and helped to guide human development. Of course, if this was true we would have to question where these aliens are now; do they live amongst us, are they watching our development? Or perhaps they have lost interest and moved onto another world. It is even possible that humans have not developed in the way they expected and they have changed their focus to a new project.

The alien astronaut theory includes the idea that aliens are the ones who are actually responsible for building the pyramids and the Easter Island heads. It may be that they provided the tools to allow humans to finish the job and even the plans to build from. Of course, this is all simply conjecture; there is no concrete evidence that aliens have been to Earth before. There are a variety of gaps in the history and development of Earth; these have been pointed out by a variety of people as indications of alien involvement in the development of human life. There are also incidents of artefacts being discovered which appear to either be out of context with what is known about a certain time period or to be considered beyond the capabilities of human development at a given point in time. Of course, it is possible that these gaps in human history are not in any way related to the existence of aliens. Both sides of the argument rely on their own hypothesis; there is no d data to prove or disprove any of the claims. It is this that makes it impossible to stop people theorising that aliens have visited Earth in the past.

In fact, this type of theory is actually gaining in popularity as even scientists now admit that it is highly likely that other intelligent life exists in the universe. NASA has even confirmed they fully expect to find alien life within the next few years; although they stop short of saying it has already visited Earth. The assumption that there must be other alien life lends credence to the idea that aliens have visited in the past. They may have a policy of non-interference which a few of them ignored by trying to guide humanity. It may even be possible that a few arrived with their own intentions and were happy to rule humanity like gods; until others intervened and removed them. All of these theories are plausible, but they are just theories. The facts regarding alien contact are few and far between and have often be distorted when represented in the science fiction novels and theories of the early twentieth century. Surprisingly, despite our rapidly increasing knowledge we have not yet got any closer to the truth concerning aliens and their involvement on Earth.

There are many figurines and similar artefacts that have survived through the years. Many of these pieces do not appear to have been based on the look of a human; this leads to a range of theories regarding the images actually being created as representations of alien visitors to the planet. One fact which does arise from these ancient artefacts is the similarities in certain stories. It has been established for many years that the sooner an event is recorded after it has happened, the more accurate the detail will be. This premise is as true today as it was in ancient times. It then becomes interesting that there are several stories of a being in Sumerian history which is seen to resemble, in some ways, a fish. This being is said to have taught the Sumerians mathematics, the arts and even advanced agricultural methods. What makes these tales intriguing is that they have been recorded by different people and yet the details are remarkably similar. This suggests either a collaboration for an unknown purpose, or points at several parties telling the same story from their own, personal point of view. Unfortunately much of the Sumerian language remains unknown even today, making it very difficult to confirm the authenticity of these tales.

A step forward in time to modern society and we are still unable to prove or disprove the existence of these extraterestial beings. However, there remains a question over the traditional view of an alien. Many of the images used by modern society when discussing the potential of alien life and how it might look, bear uncanny resemblances to the figurines which were made thousands of years ago. The question is whether our image of aliens today stems from the preconceived images of the past, or whether there is a genuine link between these visualisations; one that would most likely be alien in origin.

This point links with the conspiracy theory which has developed and argues that an alien intervention in the past is the only logical conclusion with the facts available to us. The theory suggests that the government is aware of this but chooses to cover up the fact by producing its own version of events; which is simply accepted as true.

According to the history books Columbus was the first person to cross the Atlantic and it took him just sixty days. This suggests that, in all the thousands of years which humans have been on the planet before Columbus took his epic voyage, not one soul managed to cross the Atlantic. Yet, the mighty civilisations of ancient Egypt, Sumer and Rome had the capability to sail anywhere. It seems unlikely that the sheer curiosity of man never took anyone else past the fifty nine day mark. Even if everyone believed the world to be flat you would expect there to be tales of people disappearing into the distance to find the edge of the world.

This theory is further compounded by the fact there exists some remarkable similarities between the cultures which developed in America and mainland Europe; it seems highly unlikely that two independent cultures would emerge with similar values and beliefs without ever having been aware of each other's existence. This fact is confirmed by the Egyptians and the Peruvians. Both these groups of people believed in the idea of reincarnation; that your soul is immortal and appears in a new body once your old one has died. Both of these groups are also known to worship the sun and the moon, and even the stars in the sky. Whilst this type of worship may simply be a logical extension of the world around them combined with a primitive belief structure, it does not explain why both cultures built pyramids. In fact both the Egyptian pyramids and the Peruvian used massive rocks which even modern day cranes would not be able to lift!

The similarities between the cultures continue in the embalming and mummification of their dead the fact that both cultures wrapped their children's heads to elongate the skull. It is believed this was done to allow people to reach a higher state of consciousness. Even the year was divided into twelve months and the idea of animal sacrifice was common on both continents. Even the practice of the King ploughing the first furrow was mimicked on both sides of the Atlantic. It seems highly unlikely that it was possible for these two civilisations to arise with such similarities and no record of any contact between them.

The symbols used by the ancient Mexicans include the cross and the swastika; both of these are seen as European symbols and yet they were included in the creation of the Olmec temples; even the lion god hieroglyph appears in both cultures. The same is true in reverse; examples of Mexican influences abound in ancient Egypt. These range from the Mayan arts and glyphs to the discovery of two thousand year old art on both continents which show the merging of all species of human kind; despite the fact that these cultures supposedly did not meet until much more recently. Even the language which formed part of these two civilisations has a shared influence. The current day Mayan's can recognise and read most of the language of their ancestors, as can the Egyptians. But, they can also understand much of each other's language!

There are many more examples of how these two civilisations, who supposedly never met, have approached life in exactly the same way. Both cultures are known to have used bricks and cement; there are plenty of examples of how advanced their architecture was and the fact that both cultures used similar materials to create roads, suspension bridges and even huge temples. It is also true that both cultures mined gold, silver, tin and a variety of other metals; they engaged in painting, sculpting and even adopted similar techniques for ploughing and farming the ground. Perhaps most telling is that both of these civilisations devoted their time to creating massive sailing boats and fashioned similar appearing swords, bows and arrows, slings and even spears.

The list of similarities can be continued almost indefinitely; leaving you with very little option but to believe that there must have either been some external influence guiding both societies, or, that there was interaction between the cultures. The idea that these civilisations expanded and flourished with the same basic ideas suggests a common influence. It is already widely accepted that two cultures that have similar origins will produce similar customs and traditions. This theory simply suggests the reverse is true; two cultures with similar beliefs and structure must have originated from the same being and ideology.

Another interesting fact, which adds to the weight behind a potential conspiracy, is that all historical and government produced material concerning the ancient Sumerian, Egyptian and even Babylonian civilisations refers to civilisations which arose from nowhere. All of these civilisations appear to have arrived at the peak of their prowess. There are no records of their progression and growth, simply a civilisation which appeared and flourished. It has been suggested that the Sumerian texts refer to older cities, such as Atlanta and that this confirms these places existed before the Sumerian's arrival. The conclusion to this theory is that the Sumerian's were actually a 'lost civilisation' which relocated. Unfortunately, the texts in Sumerian do not confirm that this was the case, they simply refer to famous cities; it is impossible to tell if they are talking about places which existed in their time or in some other context.

As well as arising from nowhere, all of these mighty civilisations appear to have slowly decayed. The Sumerians were incredibly advanced for their period in history; they had courts, impressive buildings and an entire legal system as well as the arts and culture. However, their arrival was the peak of their advancement; future generations used less advanced building techniques and had less culture! It has been suggested that this is because the advancements in civilisation were given to the Sumerians by aliens, the inability of the human mind to grasp the knowledge and improve upon it at that stage, meant that the techniques and skills were largely lost. Yet, this is the same culture that gave us the modern concept of time, mathematics and even space, medicine and a variety of the arts. It seems amazing to think that all these developments simply arrived from nowhere and the people who created them simply declined in skills and power.

The logical conclusion is that these people were either from another planet or were given these skills and techniques by beings from another world. The reason why these beings would wish to help humans is unclear; it may be simply a small gift to repay humanity for their assistance (natural resources) in repairing a space craft; it may even be that the civilisation was created by aliens who were marooned here; until such time as they were rescued. What is certainly true is that there are questions which remain unanswered; either there is a conspiracy to keep the real truth hidden, or we may never know what really happened and how these civilisations came into being. The history we know of these ancient civilisations could be true, it could be a conspiracy to hide the existence of aliens, or it could simply be a distortion of facts and stories throughout the ages; deliberate or otherwise.

CHAPTER 4 – GILGAMESH; THE DEMI-GOD

The epic of Gilgamesh is a collection of stories which surround the fifth king of Sumer. It was written sometime between 2150 BC and 1400BC and is considered to be the oldest epic piece of western literature in existence. The fifth king, Gilgamesh was supposed to have been the descendent of Lugalbanda (the priest king), and, Ninsun; a goddess, holy mother and great queen. The fact that she was a god made Gilgamesh a demi-god; he is believed to have possessed an amazing, beyond human strength and longevity. Records show that his time as king was one hundred and twenty six years; an impressive feat by today's standards!

The tales of his deeds were recorded in this epic as he became an inspiration to all those around him. Stories stretched across the land of his divine status and the amazing range of his abilities. He appeared in a variety of heroic stories and poems from this period; it is generally agreed that the first of these tales shows the respect which was awarded to him. The story goes that the goddess of love and war, Inanna, planted a tree so that when it grew she would be able to make a chair and a bed from it. However a snake infests its roots, a demon it centre and an Anzu bird its branches! Her brother Utu, who is the god of the sun, refuses to help her. However, Gilgamesh comes to kill the snake, at which point both the demon and the Anzu bird leave the tree. He then chops the trunk and presents it to Inanna to allow her to make her chair and bed.

The stories continue, they centre around the theme that the gods believed Gilgamesh to be arrogant and proud. To teach him the value of humility they send a great warrior called Enkidu to defeat him. However, despite a huge fight neither is able to beat the other; instead they become friends. They then undertake a range of adventures together until Enkidu dies. His death is said to have been ordered by the gods to punish Gilgamesh and Enkidu for their actions. They are said to have killed Humbaba; the guardian of Cedar Mountain. They also killed the bull of heaven who is sent to punish Gilgamesh because he was not interested in the goddess Ishtar. Enkidu's death creates the realisation in Gilgamesh that all beings are mortal and he then seeks the meaning of life and a way to withstand death. The stories eventually show his death and continued existence as a judge in the afterlife. He may have passed on but his actions are available for all eternity.

It is certainly very likely that Gilgamesh actually existed. Alongside the stories, he appears in the King list and is mentioned by several other Kings; of other countries. He is believed to have built the great walls of Uruk and, as recently as 2003, a team of archaeologists believed they had discovered his tomb. Their dig discovered evidence of a variety of structures which include the tomb; these structures are all described in the Epic of Gilgamesh.

It is generally accepted that the epic is built around original short Sumerian stories and poems. These have been merged to create a complete story. Unfortunately, it has not been possible to translate all the tablets and there remain several gaps in the stories. Even modern computers have been unable to translate all the texts. Although this is considered to be the first example of great western literature, the fact that it is still studied and so well known today should make you question why; after all, there are many excellent examples of literature which have not been studied to the extent this one has. There are two main versions of this epic tale; the standard Akkadian version and the Old Babylonian version. Both of these versions are actually compilations of the original texts and there are different starts to the books. The Babylonian version sees Gilgamesh as a king who was better than any king before him. However, the Akkadian version refers to Gilgamesh's meeting with Uta-Napishti and how he was shown the right way to worship the god, why death is important and important facts about living a good life; as a person and a king.

Each of the original stories which are included in this epic first appeared on a tablet. Although many of them cannot be fully translated or they are incomplete, there is enough of each story left to provide the general outline. The actual tale can be enhanced through studying other records of this period in time.

It is interesting to note that the Sumerians predated Christ and yet many of the stories have similarities to those which are found in the bible. For instance, the Garden of Eden is mentioned at the start of the bible; it is also referred to many times in Sumerian texts. The basic concept of humans falling out of paradise by displeasing God is valid in both cultures. The book of Ecclesiastes refers to a triple-stranded rope; this also appears in the epic. The flood in the bible is also referred to in the Gilgamesh Epic. In fact, the story is almost identical; the name of the hero may be different but the premise, instructions to build an ark and the outcome are all the same.

This leads to an interesting question regarding the civilisations of this period. Through a separate process these two societies came to believe in god and that worshipping him or them; would ensure their survival and prosperity. The tale in itself is not remarkable however the likenesses suggest that the writers of the bible drew inspiration from the existing stories and tales. This then means that the biblical stories which are part of the foundation of Christianity are actually based on the stories of an earlier period and not divine intervention. Although these stories are included in the Old Testament and are not an essential part of the foundations of Christianity it does raise questions regarding the history and origins of Christianity. There are those that support the theory that all religions started from one source; alien encounters.

This theory may not be as far-fetched as it seems. There is very little dispute that the ancient civilisations which existed on this planet worshipped the sun and the stars; quite simply it was a force which seemed more powerful and mysterious than anything which existed on earth; particularly to early humans who had a limited understanding of the world around them. The natural progression of this belief is to assume that these heavenly forces visit the planet and have a profound effect on it. Whilst this may be alien arrivals, it may also be explained in a simpler manner; such as shooting stars, comets and other astronomical incidents.

Without being able to understand these events, it is natural to build your own version of what has occurred and this gradually becomes seen as the truth. If this is coupled with a lack of any scientific explanation otherwise you will see the beginnings of the gods and their individual powers. This will generate a wealth of stories, which will culminate in demi-gods and arguments between the gods. Each of these stories will almost certainly be based on an element of truth, such as an incredible, god-like feat.

The fact that the stories of these feats and the punishments that have been issued by the gods appear in several different religious texts; albeit in slightly different formats, suggests that all the religions actually stem from one point. Subsequent, god like astronomical occurrences spark new religions.

If this theory is to be believed then it is likely that Gilgamesh was simply a human king, who lived for much longer than most people at that time and appeared to have superhuman strength. His legacy has been exaggerated each time it has been told but the basic premise is true. The fact that there have been enough artefacts recovered to confirm his existence makes this a real possibility. However, combining these stories with the advanced technology, culture and knowledge of both the solar system and the arts does give credence to the possibility that these stories have originated from the arrival of aliens on Earth. After all, modern historians and governments seem content to leave history as it is; without delving into the arrival of these civilisations and their gradual demise. This may imply that not only have aliens visited this planet but that the world powers are aware of this fact and are doing their best to keep this fact hidden from society. This theory continues today in the form of area 51 and other significant potential alien encounters.

The Gilgamesh tablets and the texts they contain are thousands of years old, yet this period is responsible for many of the modern day conventions, particularly our method of calculating time. There would seem to be a high level of probability that there is more than just a grain of truth to the suggestion that alien beings were in some way responsible for the leaps in technology, civilisation and the subsequent rise of many of the religions found around the world. It is impossible to tell whether these beings intentionally moved humanity forward or this was simply a side effect of their presence. What is certain is that Gilgamesh existed and the stories surrounding him and the other gods could very easily refer to the existence of an alien species.

CHAPTER 5 – BABYLONIA; THE NEXT CHAPTER?

The land of the Sumerians is known as Sumer because their neighbours and rivals, the Akkadians called their land this. The fact that the Akkadians took over the Sumerian land means that it is their name for the land which has been passed down through the generations. However, the Sumerians actually referred to their land as simply kiengi; which means the land! Records show they are the oldest civilisation in what is now known as Iraq and potentially the oldest in the world.

When the Akkadians took over the lands of the Sumer, approximately three thousand eight hundred years ago, they effectively created the next generation of civilisation. Their name for these people was Babili which translates as the gates of gods. However, the Greeks later corrupted this word and called the area Babylonia; a name which has stuck until the present day. It is worth noting that the Akkadians did not conquer this area; they simply took it over after the decline of the Sumerians.

Babylonia is listed as the heir to the Sumerian empire. In fact, history suggests that the Babylonia Empire was created slowly after the Sumerian and Akkadian empires had been destroyed by the Elamites. The Elamites were a fierce fighting force who simply liked to destroy and take anything they could. Although they were not interested in building an empire or controlling the Akkadian one; their actions disrupted the power balance and helped to cause the demise of the Akkadian empire. In all the chaos the small city of Babili established itself as an independent state and started to cautious stretch its grip on the region around it.

It is estimated that this slow encouragement on other lands happened over a century; at this point the leader of the Babylonian empire, Hammurabi stepped up their efforts. His kingdom was central to Mesopotamia; with the aid of a well trained army he took control over the entire region by force. The empire quickly grew to be thousands of miles wide. Hammurabi, however, had a lot in common with the Sumerians who had come before him. He did not simply want to own all the land; he wanted to improve the lives of all who lived on it and encourage the growth of the arts and culture. Copying the format of the Sumerians he created a central government, rebuilt the roads and cleared the canals; allowing water to flow again and trade to open up across the land. Of course, these actions included taxing the population. He was considered to be a priest king and intrinsically linked with deities. In addition he made sure that Babylonia was seen as the holiest city and that all future kings would need to be crowned there. Even more impressive was his creation of the code of laws. It is believed that these were based upon the code of Ur Nammu; this was the code of conduct or law of the land created by the Sumerian Empire.

In many ways it would appear that Hammurabi wanted to replicate the Sumerian empire, the structure of the Babylonia Empire was incredibly similar, in both terms of the laws, social structure and their beliefs. In fact, many of the subsequent empires which appeared after Babylonia continued these Sumerian traditions. This is generally believed to be because the Sumerian empire was so impressive that all future empires tried to emulate it. However, it is also a fact that the Babylonian reconstruction of the Sumerian empire meant that this structure, civilisation and way of life continued for many years to come. Perhaps the achievements of the Sumerian empire would not be part of modern life without the intervention of the Babylonians! The Babylonians, along with the subsequent generations continued to build their homes with mud bricks, their palaces and other buildings continued to be built in the same vein as the original Sumerian designs. Whilst it is possible that this is because stone was not in plentiful supply, it is interesting to note that this trend continued long after it was easy to acquire and move stone. Whether there were believed to be more benefit in building with mud as opposed to stone, or if this was simply a cultural legacy it is difficult to say with any certainty.

What is particularly interesting is why the Babylonians expended so much energy and resources emulating the Sumerian empire. In fact, this period of history shows very little sign of new innovations. This may be because the Sumerian style of government and structure was more than adequate for the needs of these people. However, if this was true then it would be logical to see an improvement in the arts and culture of the period; this does not appear to have happened. It, therefore, leaves the question of whether the Babylonians were actually the Sumerians; simply biding their time before rebuilding their empire.

The Babylon Empire survived from 1800 BC to 539 BC. This period is split into two dynasties. The first, as established by Hammurabi, existed for approximately two hundred years. After this time the empire was conquered by several other forces; all neighbours of the huge empire. After several hundred years of control, a Babylonian king, Nebuchadnezzar, took back control of the empire by defeating the invaders and driving them out of the empire. In the process he used a local tribe, the Chaldeans; they assisted with his rule and the empire thrived for over a thousand years in peace. The fact that Nebuchadnezzar took control is not surprising; he was an ambitious king who wanted the best for his people. However, his reign continued the earlier Babylonian traditions and beliefs; all of which were based upon the Sumerian way of life. Again, the question arises as to why was the Sumerian way of life so important to these people?

The Babylonians continued to believe in the God Marduk and modern science shows that the Chaldeans developed a deeper understanding of astrology and the universe around them. This is not surprising as this was simply a continuation of the beliefs and work of the Sumerians. However, there is also a theory which suggests that Babylon was much more than just a rebuilt version of the Sumerian empire.

As the Babylon civilisation based its beliefs and practices on the Sumerian way of life it is not surprising that they are a variety of symbols which are prevalent in both periods. These symbols include the Sumerian omega symbol which originally had curvy lanes, although the Greeks later changed this to straight lines. In Sumerian culture the wavy lines are supposed to represent water. The symbol was often linked with the chariot of the gods and many interpret the lines between the chariot and the omega to represent the power the gods had to extend life or even grant immortality. This symbol along with many others was present in the Babylonian period as well as the Sumerian one. It is believed to be linked with the gods, and these gods were actually the alien beings which have been referred to in many hypotheses as the Anunnaki.

It is believed by some that a brotherhood was formed in Babylonia which still exists today. The founders of this group are the gods which the Sumerians worshipped; all of which met in Babylonia after the great flood has passed. In fact, it is possible that Babylonia is actually older than the Sumerian cities and it is responsible for the Sumerian people and their legacy to modern humanity. Of course, despite there being some evidence which suggests Babylon may be much older than first thought, it is impossible to say if this theory is true or not. What is true is that the Babylonians and the

Sumerians made huge contributions towards modern society and the beliefs, religious and otherwise, which are still held to be true today. In fact, many of the deities which were in existence during this period can be found to be part of the main religions still practiced today. A good example of this is Queen Semiramis, symbolised as a fish, a symbol which remains intrinsically important to the Christian religion. In addition to this, Queen Semiramis is also known as a dove, a symbol which appears in a multitude of places around the world; including the sceptre of the British Queen and the political arm of the IRA!

This belief and theory continues that the brotherhood which was originally formed in the Sumerian and Babylonian times is not only in existence today but is the most influential organisation in the world. They effectively control every aspect of modern life. This is partly possible through the use of these symbols; common symbols which are used everywhere and appear harmless actually have a deeper meaning to members of this organisation. Every symbol is reversed, for example the dove generally means peace, to the Babylon brotherhood it means death and destruction. The idea that an ancient civilisation can have such an impact on modern life may seem ludicrous. However, it is interesting to note that the Babylonians always held rites to mark the starting of spring. These included buns with a solar cross; a symbol which is now firmly entrenched with the Christian Easter celebrations.

This theory is provided with more credibility by the fact that the pope's chair was made in the ninth century and is decorated with twelve plates. Each of these plates shows one of the labours of Hercules, the ancient god. It has also been claimed that Hercules was simply another name for Nimrod before he became a Greek god. Nimrod is said to be the father of Babylon, he is thought to have been a mighty tyrant and is believed to have built the Baalbek in Lebanon;

despite it consisting of three, eight hundred ton stones! Nimrod is not just visible in the Babylonian and Sumerian texts; he appears in the Bible.

Whichever way you look at the history and theories surrounding the ancient city of Babylonian, it is perfectly possible that it was more than just the capital city of an empire; its links with the modern world and the most important events of the past make it key to the development of life as we now it; whether through alien intervention or not.

Conclusion

There is no doubting that the Sumerians were a mighty civilisation, the fact that they are known as the civilised kings pertains to the technological, cultural and structural advances they made. These set the standard by which civilisations for many years to come, including modern civilisations; establish and judge themselves by. What also appears to be true, as there is no explanation or evidence to suggest otherwise, is that the Sumerians appeared from nowhere and their civilisation seemed to be preformed. In fact, in accordance with several of the other mighty civilisations, they appeared at their peak and then declined over a period of time before disappearing. The time to decline may vary between civilisations but the end result seems inevitable.

It is difficult to understand why these civilisations arrived like this and declined, it is even possible that they simply subsided and then reappeared in the future as a new civilisation. Of course, for this to be true it is necessary to believe that either some beings were capable of living for an extended period of time or that the practices, technologies and culture was passed between generations in secret until the right opportunity presented itself to re-establish power.

In fact, if you believe that this is a possible and acceptable approach it is only a small step to believing that the descendants of these great cities are still alive today and could be part of a secret society which effectively controls the world. The alternative is that the Sumerian civilisation simply appeared, made several immensely significant contributions towards humanities development and the vanished. Whilst this is possible; it would not be the first civilisation to have achieved this, it seems unlikely that a civilisation not conquered would simply vanish without any resistance. History confirms that the Sumerians existed and that they recorded many things, although the majority of these cannot be translated yet as the Sumerian language has not been mastered in modern times. This leaves a question as to why the Sumerians disappeared and yet every race after them emulated their methods; their lasting impact on humankind is a testimony to the fact that they were ahead of their time.

The alternative to these theories and beliefs is that the Sumerians were actually aliens, or created by aliens to support them. This would explain why they disappeared; their task on Earth was completed. It would also explain the re-emergence of similar civilisations. Either intelligent humans saw the possibilities in their ideas or the aliens returned for additional resources or some other reason. If there is any truth in this theory it seems highly likely that modern man would be aware of their existence. As such the only way of preventing media hysteria would be for the governments to conspire to ensure the average person is not privy to this information.

UFO and alien conspiracy theories abound in our modern world; many people believe it is simply not possible for aliens not to be amongst us. If this is the case then the theory behind Sumer and the alien gods is almost certain to be true. However, as with most good theories, it is incredibly difficult to find sufficient evidence to support any claim. There is a tablet which was located in the ancient city of Nippur which expresses the belief that the visiting aliens were here to mine for resources, possibly gold. The aliens found the job tedious and hard work so created man to do the work for them. The issue with this tablet is that its interpretation is subject to personal preference. As the ancient Sumerian language has not yet been fully translated it is not possible to be one hundred percent accurate regarding the meaning of any of the Sumerian texts. One interpretation is that aliens were responsible. Another is simply that the Sumerians worshipped the same things as many other civilisations of that period in history.

What is interesting is that there remain many unsolved puzzles relating to this period in time and the Sumerians contribution towards modern society. The majority of historians have no interest in examining the events of this time period in any further detail. This either suggests that they do not believe they will be able to find anything new, or, that they are reluctant to examine this period further; maybe this is because they have been warned to leave this period alone.

This book has been designed to help you understand the historic and cultural significance of the Sumerians and how their influence affected the world around them both then and now. The fact that this advanced civilisation has been linked with an alien arrival is not surprising; it is incredibly likely that alien life will be found. However, if aliens were responsible for the Sumerians and the subsequent Babylonians you will, once again, be asking yourself the question of where are they now? You may also wish to consider why they decided to intervene in human history at this point.

Even if you put the alien theories aside, you will quickly realise that the Sumerians had a huge impact on life; both then and now. However, with the limited information which is currently available, it is impossible to tell whether this great civilisation, with a vast an impressive knowledge of the solar system, simply developed quietly and appeared to come into existence from nowhere, or whether there is something more to their arrival and subsequent decline in power. What is true is that the civilisation really did exist and that they discussed things which should have been beyond their capabilities.

There is no way that they could have known how many planets are in our solar system and yet they seem to have this information; a lucky guess or something more mysterious? Only you can decide how you feel about these questions, the facts available and whether the truth about the Sumerians is much more complicated than it first appears.

Made in the USA
Lexington, KY
23 March 2018